I love you because when I need help you are always there.

ROBERT TAYLOR, AGE 9

I love you because you love me. I think you're a wonderful dad and you always will be. I love you Dad because you work so hard. I love you dad because you always give in on punishments and you give me sweets. I am writing this letter to try and say I love you and I always will. Louise xxx

LOUISE MELTZER, AGE 10

My dad is not a particularly famous person with money pouring in, but is more of a hard worker with a big heart.

MICHAEL KORN, AGE 10

All my love   Sophie xxx. ♡

gentle and squashy

I love you the most when you are a big softy.

CLAUDIA BOSWORTH, AGE 7

A father is a person who makes you feel wanted, when nobody else does.

DEBBIE WERNSTEIN, AGE 10

My dad is always gentle and squashy.

AMANDA FISHBURN, AGE 9

Dear Dad, I have got 2,000 reasons why I love you. I will only tell you one of them because it would take forever.
It is because you are the kindest person I know.

LUCY BURN, AGE 8

My father means to me a very warm and close feeling.

DAVID

My Daddy is
the best because
he tickles
me gently sophie
age 5

SOPHIE BARBER
AGE 5

ONAIZA AHMAD
AGE 5

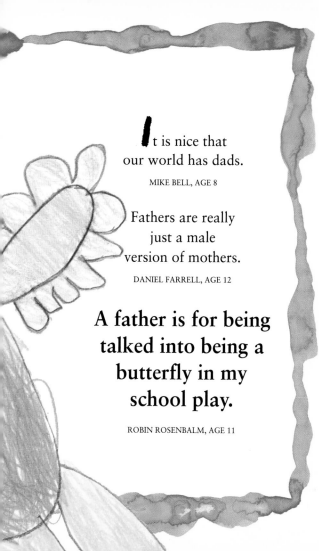

It is nice that
our world has dads.

MIKE BELL, AGE 8

Fathers are really
just a male
version of mothers.

DANIEL FARRELL, AGE 12

A father is for being talked into being a butterfly in my school play.

ROBIN ROSENBALM, AGE 11

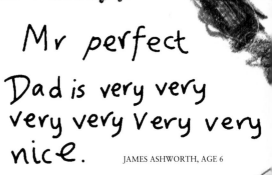

Mr perfect

Dad is very very very very Very very nice.

JAMES ASHWORTH, AGE 6

My dad's the best dad.
He's exciting.
He's adventurous.
He's super.
My dad's the best dad.

ALAN GREEN, AGE 9

JENNA LOWE, AGE 5

I f you give me one thousand million to change my mind I'd not do such a thing 'cos my dad's the world's best.

JOHANNA DAVIS, AGE 9¹/₂

And he thinks he's Mr. Perfect, so do I.

SIOBHAN, AGE 7

Dear Dad, Who says going to school doesn't teach you anything? On the many trips I have in the car with you on the way to school I have learnt more than I could doing any university course. Thanks for everything, love from me!

HAYLEY PINKERFIELD, AGE 10

Thank you especially for being there when I don't understand something.

REBECCA LAMPE, AGE 9

I like my dad when I get the "working hard badge" for my birthday.

KARA JAMES

Dad, I love you when I get good marks at school and you say, "Well Done".

CARLEY, AGE 7

MYRON YEARWOOD, AGE 10

Sarah
Bluck
age 8

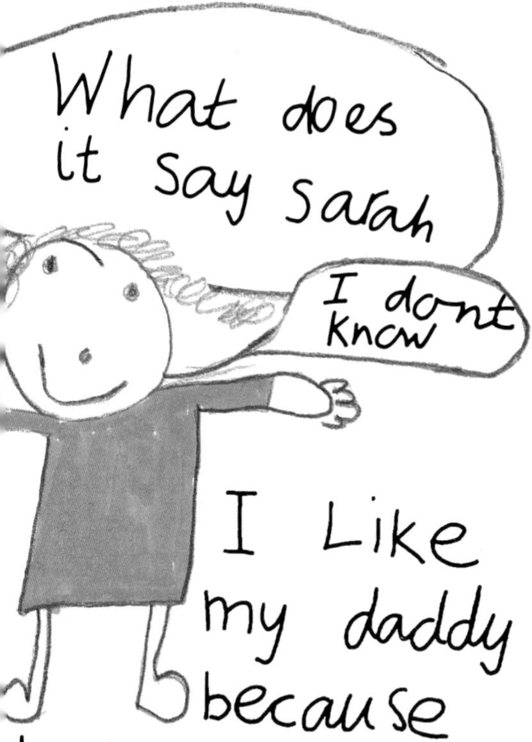

I Like my daddy because he helPs me with my home Work

SUZANAH
OCCARDI,
AGE 4

When my dad goes away I cry and cry.

CHRISTOPHER GLEGHORN, AGE 6

If I did not have my dad I would never come out of my bedroom again.

LIBBY HOLMES, AGE 8

Dear Jesus, please help my dad to stop smoking and please take care of him.

JOHN

PIPPA HURST-BROWN

NAM BUI
AGE 8¾

My best friend.

My dad is good fun to play a game with because I always beat him.

TIMOTHY READE, AGE 9

I like my dad, because when I was five he would play football.
But now he can't play football, because he's thirty.

THERON CARNELL, AGE 9

Nicolas
Rastelli

8 years Old

Some bad habits

A dad is normally found reading
a newspaper or watching sport
on television.

CLAIRE GALESKI, AGE 12

A dad is someone who watches
TV while he's sleeping.

MYRNA KNUTSON, AGE 8

A dad is somebody who can get away
with doing things he tells you not to do.

PAUL RAICHE, AGE 14

He shaves his beard
in the sink and my
mam gets sick of him

ROBERT HARRIS

JAMIE HENDERSON
AGE 8

ABIGAIL
MOSHREF
AGE 7

Little Monsters

Why does Dad put up with me?

DAVID SULLY, AGE 12

I'm a little devil. My parents are
unfortunate to have me. I always want
something, greed is my problem.
I have always been like this, since the day I
was born, but they always put me first
whatever the problem.

CLARE WILLIS, AGE 10

I think you should
win the award
because you care and
you spoil me rotten

SIAN FITZPATRICK

My protector

He keeps us safe like a brick wall!

TOBY GUTIERREZ, AGE 11

I love you because you put plasters on me when I'm hurt.

VANESSA COPPOCK, AGE 9½

A father tells us not to be scared, there is no such thing as a green-haired bear.

GINA FIGLIOLA, AGE 10

I love you Daddy because when the big boys come, I can hide behind you.

ADRIAN MARIAPPA, AGE 5

My dad throws me up in the air and he throws me high and he never drops me

Kerry age6

JESSICA ROBINSON

Daddy, I will always love you, I will always love my family as well, but there is something special I want to say about you. If you are not working for my education and many other things you are at home listening to my troubles and caring for me. Daddy, I'm sorry for when I have done wrong and Daddy, I love you.

CAROLINE ESPEY, AGE 9

You look after the family and you see that we have all we need. You work hard for us.

DANIEL HOPLEY, AGE 10

CHARLOTTE AITKEN
AGE 7

CAROLINE
WALTON,
AGE 7

Thank you for caring for me.
Thank you for cuddles.
Thank you for being friends.
Thank you for loving me.

REBECCA O'REILLY, AGE 7

My dad always reads me bedtime stories.
When I am going to sleep, he has to
read every book until I am asleep. Thank
you Dad.

SHEILA KIBUKAMUSOKE, AGE 8

Thank you Daddy for doing my bedroom.
And for listening to me when I have
problems. Thank you for loving me and
giving me money. Thank you for taking
me on holidays, for teaching me new
things every day. Thank you for
everything you have done for me.

REBECCA ROLES, AGE 8

I love you because
when I need help you
are always there.

Thank you for being
nice to me all my life.